This book
belongs
to

_____

_____

_____

Foreword

Betsy Whyte, also known as Bessie, walked a different path from most children. She was born into a family of Scottish Travellers who, when the yellow came on the broom, took to the road. Bessie was happiest during the summer months. Winters were a dreary time for the little girl who yearned for the freedom of open spaces and to walk and play once more with Ricky, her pet collie dog, among purple heather and sun-kissed meadow flowers.

With such a love of the Scottish countryside, it was no surprise to discover that when little Bessie grew up and had children of her own she would share those memories of happy summers with them. She wondered if the wider world would also like to read of her childhood; perhaps it would help people understand the Scottish Traveller way of life? Her first book became a best seller soon after publication as people clambered into bookshops to read of her magical life. *The Yellow on the Broom* became a classic, and her second book, *Red Rowans and Wild Honey,* was just as highly acclaimed.

Her great-grandson, David Pullar, had never known Bessie as he was a small child when she passed away. However, she left young David a precious legacy. To keep that legacy alive - and to celebrate what would have been her 100th birthday - he decided to create a book for children. It would be a simple, easy to read book with beautiful illustrations to honour his great-grandmother, who had given him a deep respect for the culture of her birth.

To achieve this vision, he first had to find the right artist: one who could imagine Bessie's surroundings and turn them into illustrations to bring Bessie's childhood to life. When David saw examples of Ruthie Redden's work, there was no doubt in his mind that she was the artist. As fate would have it, Ruthie was also a fan of Bessie's work. Together they have produced this wonderful book of Wee Bessie's summertime wanderings amidst the characters that gave her the memories so passionately scattered in her books. *Wee Bessie* is a beautiful book, created especially for children.

What better birthday present could a devoted great-grandson give to a woman who brought Scottish Traveller culture to life for those who knew little of it?

Jess Smith - Author and storyteller.

Wee Bessie

Written by David G Pullar
Illustrated by Ruthie Redden

HOTT PRESS

In the summer time Wee Bessie lived in a tent,
it was not very big, only a sheet covered sticks that were bent.

With Mammy Maggie, Daddy Sandy and best friend Ricky the Collie
she took to the road every summer on an adventure so jolly.

It was only time to leave when a certain yellow flower was in bloom, when buzzing bees and swirling swallows were on the zoom.

With a stubborn horse and rickety cart, they travelled the winding roads,
selling pegs and baskets, precious pearls,
and hand-me-down clothes.

They camped in ancient woodlands and beside meandering rivers
gathered twigs to light a fire for a pot of tea to stop the shivers.

By the glow of the fire and moon in the sky,
her Mammy and Daddy shared stories and songs,
they taught Wee Bessie how not to be shy.

Early in the mornings even before the mist had lifted,
Toby the policeman would come to see if they had shifted.

"Move along! Get along! You can't stop here!"
were the harsh words Wee Bessie and her parents would often hear.

But working hard and playing in fields of open air,
among other children and family, her life was still fun without a care.

With lots of juicy berries to pick
(one for the luggie and two for her belly),
soon an eager wee Bessie would feel sick.

Sadly, as the autumn leaves began to fall,
it was time for Wee Bessie to go back,
leaving the open countryside for school and winter in a flat.

The others at school called her names and were terribly mean,
so Wee Bessie would climb up a tree to cry where she couldn't be seen.

Wee Bessie longed for spring to leave the school and house,
to lie in a field of wild flowers
and listen to the whisperings of a mouse.

When Wee Bessie was sad her Daddy would always say,
"Ma Bonnie Wee Bessie, dinnae look sae gloom
I'll tak ye on the road again when the yellows on the broom."

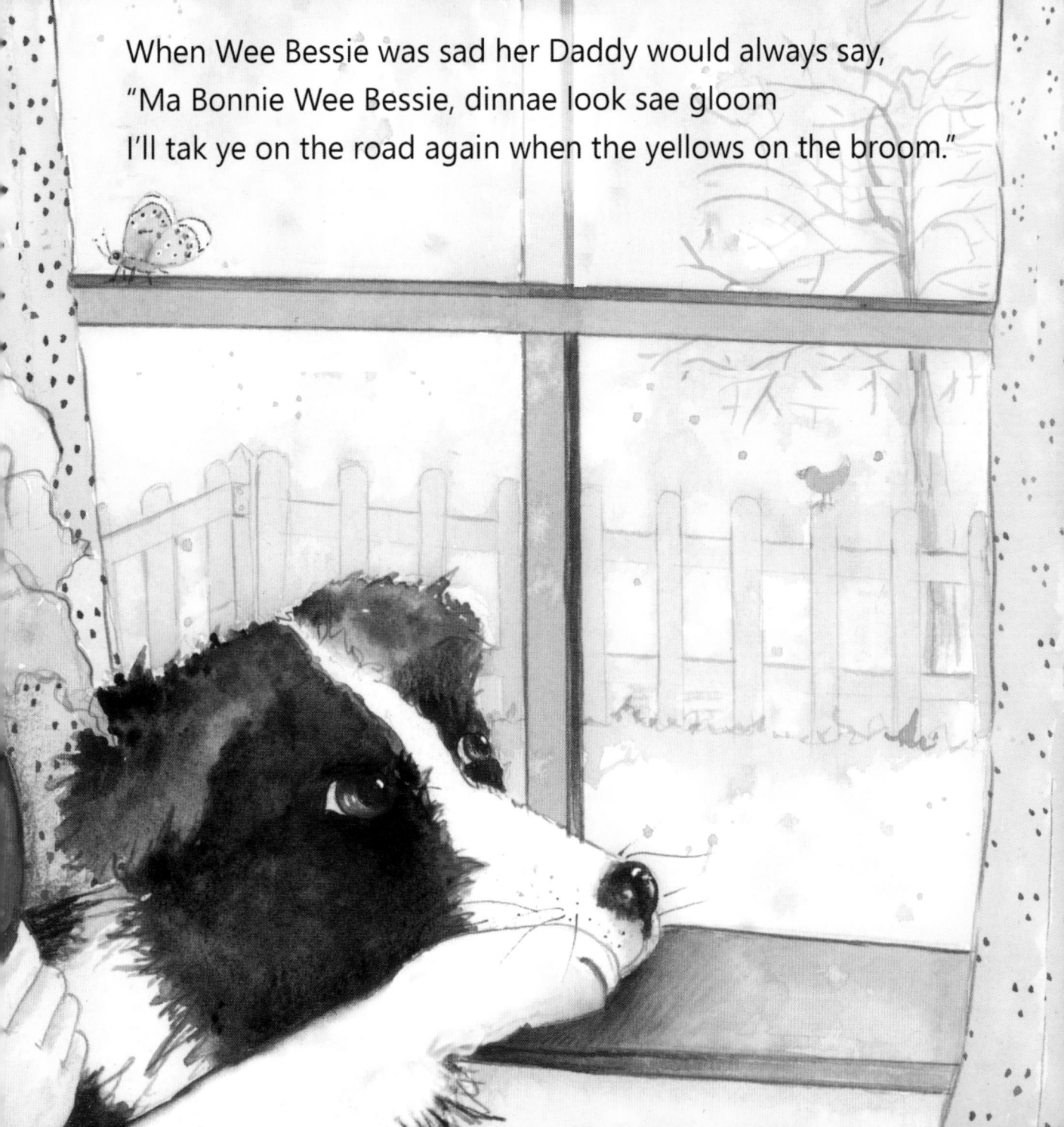

Wee Bessie loved travelling with Mammy Maggie, Daddy Sandy
and best friend Rickie the collie.
Each summer when she took to the road,
she knew she would have an adventure so jolly.

About HOTT

Heart of the Travellers HOTT is a Scottish Charitable Incorporated Organisation (SCIO) dedicated to conserving the stories, songs, genealogies and histories of Scottish Travellers. We work to promote an awareness and understanding of the roles Scottish Travellers have played in the history of Scotland through the sharing of our oral histories and culture. We celebrate the values of One Scotland, Many Cultures by contributing to the complete story of Scotland and its people.

Our cluster of dedicated individuals came into existence as a campaigning group to save and protect the Tinkers' Heart in Argyll, the only physical monument to Scottish Travellers, and through discussion we realised that our culture was in danger of being lost to the mists. We consider education as key to succeeding in our mission and believe that publications such as *Wee Bessie* help create a better understanding and recognition of our culture.

We hope that Wee Bessie inspires you to ask questions and sparks an interest in your own personal history. Who knows, you may find that you are descended from a child of the mist.

David G Pullar - Author

David G Pullar is a professional horticulturist from the tiny fishing village of Usan which sits just south of Montrose, Angus. The same village where his famous great grandmother Betsy Whyte first took a permanent house after leaving her life on the road. With the life of his great grandmother as the source of much of his inspiration; David has, since his teenage years, been showcasing the histories, traditions and customs of Scotland's Travelling people. With the wonderful stage production of his great grandmother's first book *The Yellow on the Broom,* by Anne Downie; and the song of the same name by Adam McNaughton having inspired exhibitions, festivals, songs and music what better way to introduce the life of the celebrated Scottish Traveller to a new and younger audience than through a children's book? Just like Betsy's book, *Wee Bessie* is a first of its kind in Scotland.

www.heartofthetravellers.scot

Ruthie Redden - Artist

Ruthie is an artist and illustrator based in Galloway on Scotland's beautiful wild southwest coast in the Artists town of Kirkcudbright. Through her research Ruthie explores the folklore, history and tradition rooted in Scotland's past, much of it on the brink of being lost.

As a pictorial storyteller, Ruthie uses the narrative elements of folklore to evoke a connection to a time when we were intrinsically tied to the rhythms of Mother Nature and to inspire interest in our rich Scottish heritage.

We asked Ruthie about her involvement with Wee Bessie she responded by saying -

Every so often I come across a book that has a deep effect on me, 'The Yellow on the Broom' was such a book and has long been a favourite. As I read Bessie's story all those years ago, I saw the world through her eyes. I felt a deep connection with her love of country ways and her need to lose herself in the wild places. My work is inspired by the very same thing and I feel honoured to have been given the task of bringing both David's and Bessie's words to life through my illustrations.

www.ruthieredden.com

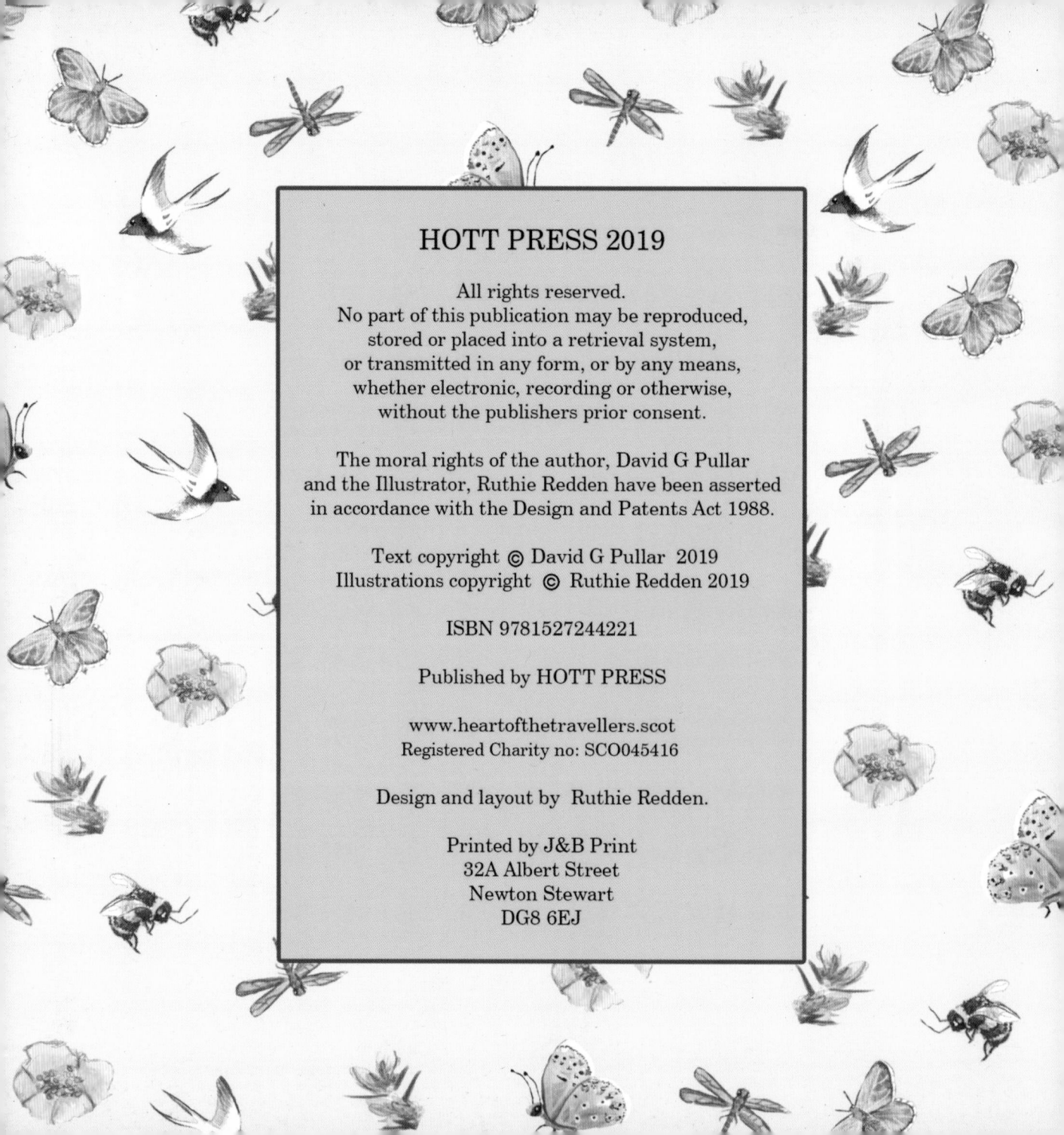

ISBN 9781527244221

Published by HOTT PRESS

www.heartofthetravellers.scot
Registered Charity no: SCO045416

Design and layout by Ruthie Redden.

Printed by J&B Print
32A Albert Street
Newton Stewart
DG8 6EJ